ME AND MY HORSE

The Big Event

Toni Webber

COPPER BEECH BOOKS
Brookfield, Connecticut

© Aladdin Books Ltd 2002

Produced by:
Aladdin Books Ltd
28 Percy Street
London W1T 2BZ

ISBN 0-7613-2851-3

First published in the United States in 2002 by:
Copper Beech Books,
an imprint of
The Millbrook Press
2 Old New Milford Road
Brookfield, Connecticut 06804

Editor:
Harriet Brown

Designers:
Flick, Book Design & Graphics
Simon Morse

Illustrators:
Terry Riley, Simon Morse

Cartoons: Simon Morse

Cataloging-in-Publication data is on file at the Library of Congress.

10 9 8 7 6 5 4 3 2 1

Contents

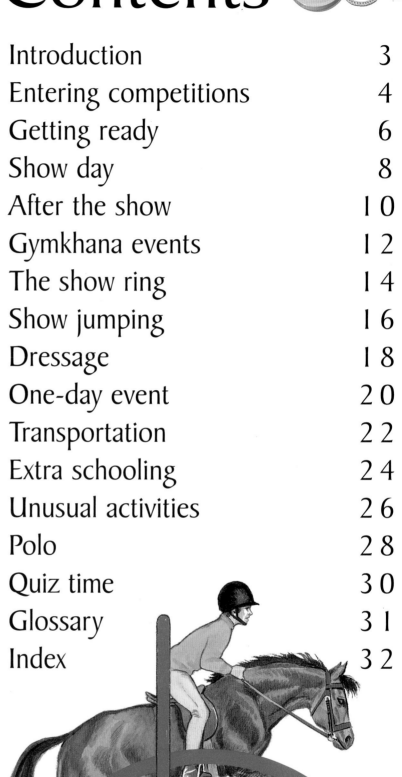

Introduction

The Big Event is a lively guide to entering competitions with your horse. Once you have mastered the basics of riding, there is likely to be a time when you start to think about competing. There are many activities you can try with your horse, from showing to dressage to gymkhana games. Most shows cater for all abilities, so you will always be competing against riders of a similar standard to you. You never know, you might just win a ribbon or two.

Competing sounds so exciting! I'd love to win a ribbon. In fact, it looks like fun whether you win or not.

Always Remember:
Look in these boxes for further information about competing with your horse. They contain important points that you should try to remember.

✔ **THE RIGHTS AND WRONGS**
Look out for these check boxes. They show you how to do things correctly. Just as important, look for the "X" boxes. These show you how not to do things. ✘

Q What are these boxes for?

A These question and answer panels are here to help answer your questions about any aspect of competing. Each panel is relevant to the subject on the rest of the page.

Wednesday
I was talking to my friends at the stable today. They were telling me that going in for competitions is their favorite way to spend school vacations. The owner of our stable even lets people rent her horses to enter shows.

Entering competitions

It is not winning but taking part that makes competing so much fun. Training your horse to meet certain standards or to tackle a difficult jumping course is very satisfying. Of course, if you place, or better still, finish first, that's a big bonus.

FIND OUT WHAT'S ON

Most organizers advertise their events in a local newspaper. Events usually fall into one of three categories—horse shows, hunter trials, or one-day events. Horse shows are a mixture of showing, jumping, and gymkhana games. Hunter trials are a cross-country competition, and one-day events include dressage, show jumping, and cross-country.

WHAT TO ENTER

First you need to get a schedule from the organizers of the classes that are going to be held. Look carefully at the classes to see which ones suit you best. A nice-looking, reliable horse that is a steady jumper may be well-suited to a Working Pony Hunter class. Show jumping is a good choice if your horse is quick, agile, and doesn't knock down fences too often. Most horses enjoy cross-country, which involves jumping solid jumps, ditches, and sometimes water. All-round ponies suit the Best Pony Club Pony class. Little, quick ponies are often good at gymkhana games, especially if you are as active as they are. Check the timing of the classes (see page 8).

Tuesday
I'm going to enter lots of shows this season. My friend Annabel says that Oscar should do the Working Pony Hunter class because he's such a safe jumper. He hardly ever knocks down any fences.

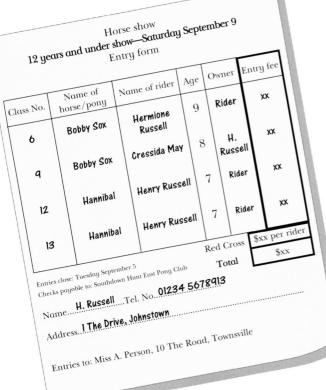

Class No.	Name of horse/pony	Name of rider	Age	Owner	Entry fee
6	Bobby Sox	Hermione Russell	9	Rider	xx
9	Bobby Sox	Cressida May	8	H. Russell	xx
12	Hannibal	Henry Russell	7	Rider	xx
13	Hannibal	Henry Russell	7	Rider	xx
				Red Cross	$xx per rider
				Total	$xx

Entries close: Tuesday September 5
Checks payable to: Southdown Hunt East Pony Club

Name...**H. Russell**...Tel. No...**01234 5678913**

Address...**1 The Drive, Johnstown**...

Entries to: Miss A. Person, 10 The Road, Townsville

FILL IN THE FORM

Every schedule should come with an entry form. You must fill in the classes you want to enter, the name of your horse and its rider, the rider's age, and the horse's owner. More than one horse or rider can be entered on the same form. Make sure that the check is completed correctly and return it with the form to the organizer before the closing date.

Always Remember:

Keep your horse interested in what it is doing. Practice makes perfect, but not if you jump the same jump over and over again. Even the happiest horse will get bored and start refusing. Try to think of exciting things for your horse to do. For example, when out hacking, jump fallen logs to add variety to your ride. It is also a good idea to ride through small streams to get your horse used to water.

HORSE FITNESS

If your horse is ridden regularly and is on the right diet, getting and keeping it fit should not be difficult. Walking and trotting up and down hills will help to build up muscle. Regular schooling will teach your horse to be obedient and help to make it flexible and responsive to your commands. If possible, have lessons with an experienced instructor. This stops bad habits from developing. If you are expecting your horse to do more exercise than usual, you may have to adjust its diet. Ask an experienced person to help you work out the right amount to feed your horse.

4 pm—I did a really good job braiding Oscar's mane once I got the hang of it. I only had to redo two braids, so I was quite pleased. I did them the night before the show and covered them with some old nylon stockings to keep them tidy.

Getting ready

The secret of having a good time at a show is one word—preparation. If you allow enough time to get both yourself and your horse ready, you will arrive at the show in the right state of mind. Here's how you do it...

Sponges

Q What grooming kit do I need to take with me?

A You will need a body brush, stable rubber, hoof pick, and hoof oil. You will also need sponges to wipe around your horse's eyes, nostrils, and dock area (under its tail). In a cross-country competition, it helps to have a water carrier and bucket, together with a large sponge, for sponging your horse down.

Hoof pick

Body brush

Q What other preparations do I need?

A It sounds obvious, but try to get a good night's sleep the night before a show. It is easy to get so excited about the next day that sleep won't come. Go to bed at your normal time, take a warm drink, have a hot bath (anything that makes you relax), set the alarm, and go to sleep. You will have a far better time if you are wide awake and thinking clearly for the competition.

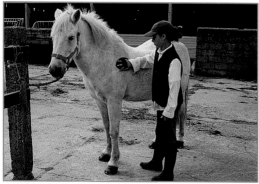

GROOMING

Grooming for a show is not very different from the grooming you give your horse every day. Any light-colored hair on your horse, such as its socks (white markings on its legs), may need special care to remove grass stains. You can use powdered chalk as extra whitening.

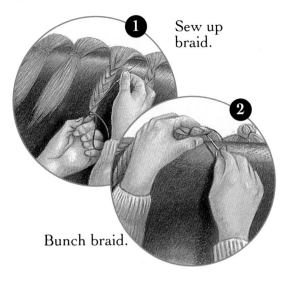

① Sew up braid.

②

Bunch braid.

BRAIDING THE MANE AND TAIL

Divide the well-brushed mane into evenly sized bunches. Tightly braid each bunch. Use a needle and thread to sew up the end (step 1, left). Turn the end under, roll it up, and stitch it firmly in place (step 2, left). For the tail, braid it from the top, drawing in hairs evenly from each side (right). Before you reach the end of the tail bone, stop drawing in side hairs and make a thin braid the length of the tail. Tuck it under to form a loop and stitch it in place.

CLEANING TACK

If you are going to clean your tack properly, you must take it apart. So it is important that you learn how to put it together again first. Wash all the metalwork in soapy water. Rinse it well and dry thoroughly. If the leather is muddy,

remove mud with a damp cloth. Rub saddle soap into the leather with a slightly damp sponge. If there is any foam at all, your sponge is too wet. You can put your saddle pads and cloth girth in the washing machine. Leather girths should be saddle-soaped.

Always Remember:

Get everything ready the night before. You do not want to have to hunt for anything just when you should calmly be eating your breakfast. Clean your jodhpur boots, brush your jacket and hat, and check that you have a clean shirt the night before the show. Have you got two riding gloves or is one still somewhere at the back of the closet, where you tossed it last time you wore it? You will still have to clean your horse, so it may help to pack all your show clothes into a carryall and take them with you to the stable. Then you can change into them once your horse is ready. Don't forget to put some money in your pocket, as well as a clean handkerchief.

I was so busy getting everything ready for the show this morning, I forgot my lunch!

Show day

This is the day you have been waiting for, and you want to enjoy every minute. If you have chosen your events carefully and allowed yourself plenty of time, it should be a memorable and fun occasion.

TIMING

At horse shows there are often many classes taking place at the same time in separate rings. If you enter a lot of classes, you may find that two of them take place at the same time. You won't be able to get your entry money back if you have to miss a class. So take care when choosing which classes to enter. It is best to allow roughly an hour for each class. If you are entering a dressage competition, you will be assigned an exact time. You should present yourself to the dressage steward at least ten minutes beforehand.

Dressage

Saturday evening

What an amazing day—my first show! I won two 3rds and a 6th, which were three ribbons more than I had hoped for. One of the thirds was in the Working Pony Hunter class and the other two ribbons were for gymkhana events. Clever, clever Oscar!

Show jumping

Lining up for the judge

Q How do I know when it is my turn to jump in a jumping class?

A The warmup ring is where you can warm up your horse before it is your turn to jump. The warmup ring steward sits at the entrance to the ring. He or she has a blackboard with the numbers of the competitors in the order that they will jump. You have to give your number to the steward. As competitors complete their rounds, the steward crosses off their numbers. Look at the blackboard, see which numbers are before you, and be ready when those competitors enter the ring.

OUTSIDE THE RING

When you get to the horse show, visit the secretary's tent and collect your number. This will be a cardboard number that is worn around your waist. At a cross-country event, your number will be on a bib or tabard, so that it is displayed front and back. You will probably be asked for a deposit for this, which you'll get back when you return your number. When you are not actually taking part in a class, make sure you don't tire out your horse or disturb other competitors and spectators by riding up and down the field.

Sunday
Before entering the jumping competition I got some practice in the clear round jumping. I paid an entry fee, did my round, and would have won a clear-round ribbon if Oscar hadn't knocked the last pole down. But it was good practice for the proper jumping competition.

Always Remember:

Smile at the judge if you are awarded a prize and say, "Thank you" when given your ribbon. When everyone has been given their ribbons, you may be asked to do a victory lap. This doesn't mean galloping madly around the arena. Instead, you should follow one another at a controlled canter. The winner usually does another lap alone, while the others leave the arena.

THE PARKING LOT

Your horse trailer should be parked so that there is enough room for your horse to be tied to the outside of it without interfering with the next trailer. If there is a long time between classes, you should give your horse a haynet. Your tack and grooming kit can be stored either inside or under the trailer. Make sure they are somewhere where your horse cannot step on them. It is best if someone can stay near the trailer all the time.

Don't leave your saddle on the ground, where it could get damaged (above). Make sure your horse is happy before chatting with your friends (right).

After the show

Evening
We sang songs all the way home from the show. The ponies must have thought we were crazy! I put Oscar in the stable and gave him some water (which he turned up his nose at) before his feed. He really enjoyed his food, and it was dark by the time he finished. I thought I should leave him in tonight, but he was really eager to get into the field. He can have a rest tomorrow.

Whether you have a good day or a disastrous one, you and your horse will both be feeling very tired. It is important to take good care of your horse while you are still at the show and also once you are back at home.

1 Sweat scraper
Use this to remove any excess sweat. It is a useful tool to have, but not an essential one.

THE END OF THE DAY

When you have finished your classes, make sure your horse is comfortable. Remove saddle and bridle, and take out studs (see p. 17). An unpicker is useful to take out the braids. If your horse is very hot, cool it down with a sponge wrung out in cold water. Put on a summer sheet or rug. Leave your horse tied to the trailer and give it a haynet. Once you are ready to leave, put on your horse's traveling gear.

4 Turn out into the field
Horses that live out should be let into their field after they've been fed and checked over.

2 Wash
After a cross-country round, your horse will be sweating hard and puffing. Use a sponge or an old towel to wipe over its body and legs with cold water.

3 Dry
Use an old towel to get rid of the water before putting on a sweat sheet.

CHECK YOUR HORSE

Back at the stable, unload your horse from the trailer and take off its tail guard and traveling boots. If you haven't already done so, take out the braids and brush out the mane and tail. In the stable, remove the rug and brush your horse with a body brush. Pay special attention to the legs. Pick out the hooves. Put on a night rug and give your horse water and a final feed. Hang up a haynet, then leave your horse in peace.

FINAL FEED

Your horse won't need more than its usual feed after a show. Extra feed can do more harm than good. Horses that live out can be given their feed before being turned out. Offer fresh water first. Your horse will roll when you put it in the field. This is its way of relaxing.

Q What sort of injuries should I look for after the show?

A Your horse is unlikely to damage itself at an ordinary horse show, especially if it has done no more than take part in a showing class, a jumping class, and a few gymkhana events. At a cross-country event, where you will have been jumping fixed fences, it is easy for your horse to knock itself. You should check its legs for any painful areas or cuts. Bad knocks will show up the next morning, so you should examine the legs for swelling and lumps. Treat minor cuts by bathing them gently in salted water. It is unlikely that there will be any serious injuries, but if there is anything you are unsure about, call your veterinarian.

Monday
Dad made me a big bulletin board for my room. At first it only had photos of Oscar on it. But now it has my three ribbons. I've written down details about the show on the back of the ribbons. Now I'll always remember when Oscar and I won them and what we won them for.

Gymkhana events

Gymkhana games are likely to be your first taste of competition. Even if you need to be led on a lead rope, you can still take part. However, most events also require a lot of skill, fitness, and riding ability, as you'll soon find out.

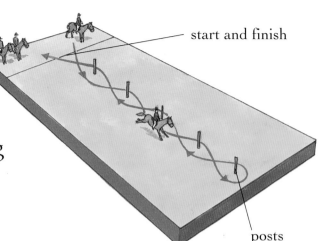

start and finish

posts

PRECISION GAMES

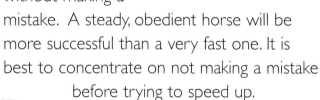

These games can involve balancing a ball on a cone or running along a line of stepping stones (right) without making a mistake. A steady, obedient horse will be more successful than a very fast one. It is best to concentrate on not making a mistake before trying to speed up.

SPEED GAMES

In these games, speed is more important than accuracy. In bending races, for example, each rider has to weave in and out of a line of barrels or posts as quickly as possible. In most races you race against other riders. The races are not timed, so to win you must finish ahead of your rivals.

Lunchtime
Annabel and I are madly practicing gymkhana games. It's more fun when we do it together, and even better when other people join in.

MIXED GAMES

These races combine precision and speed—racing to put a flag into a cone as quickly as possible, for example. All games need practice if you are to have success. You could join a Pony Club games team to improve your technique.

NECK-REINING

When you first start doing gymkhana games, you will find it difficult to control your horse without dropping equipment. You will have to practice neck-reining. Hold the reins in one hand (usually the left) and move that hand across the withers. The pressure on your horse's neck tells it which way to go. Your other hand is then free to hold the equipment.

withers

I did it! I did it! I actually managed to vault onto Oscar. The real secret is to keep Oscar moving at a brisk trot.

Q How can I practice without the proper equipment?

A You can easily make or find gymkhana equipment. Buckets, tennis balls, and old socks are easy to find. You can make an old sock bulkier by stuffing the toe with newspaper before rolling it up. For a flag, attach a scrap of cloth to a bamboo pole. Half-fill an old detergent bottle with sand for practicing the bottle race. Cones can be bought quite cheaply from hardware stores. Bean poles make good bending poles. You may be able to buy them at a garden center.

VAULTING

Some games call for the rider to get off to pick something up before remounting and riding to the finish. Races are often lost by hopping around an excited horse, with one foot in the stirrup, trying to get on. Vaulting is something anyone can do, once the technique has been learned. It's worth spending some time practicing.

Vaulting 2
Swing your right leg over the saddle. Use the hand on the saddle to steady yourself and the horse's forward movement to carry you up.

Direction of horse

Vaulting 1
Hold the reins and saddle as shown. Run beside your horse as it trots along. As the near forefoot (front foot nearest to you) hits the ground, push off with both feet and spring up.

The show ring

A showing class gives you the chance to display your horse and your riding skills. It will also let you see how your horse measures up against others. Here are a few things to remember when in a show ring.

Wednesday
I have decided that showing can be a bit boring. You spend a lot of time standing in a line doing nothing. Even so, Oscar and I entered a Best Pony Club pony showing event at the last show. It was good fun and we came in 7th out of 42 entries. It was only our first time, so I was pretty pleased!

THE SALUTE
Riders sometimes salute to tell the judge they've finished their display. To do a salute, stand squarely in front of the judge. Hold the reins in your right hand and extend your other hand straight down (above right). Bow your head at the same time.

hard hat

beige jodhpurs

tie worn with a white or pastel shirt

jacket, either tweed, black, or navy blue

polished jodhpur boots

BEHAVIOR IN THE SHOW RING
Ride around the ring at the same pace as the other riders. Leave one horse's length between you and the horse in front. Always make sure your horse looks its best; you never know when the judge is looking at you.

Thursday
I picked up lots of schedules at the last show, so Annabel and I are having fun deciding which ones to go to. Next week, there's show jumping at the Old Oaks Equestrian Center. There's even a pairs class, so the show seems just right for us.

PERFORMING A TEST

The judge may ask you to show your horse's paces. To do this, do a circuit of the ring at walk, trot, and canter. Next, canter a figure-eight. Remember to slow down to a trot before you change the rein (direction). Halt by the judge, rein back (walk backward) a few steps, and return to your place.

1 Warming up
You should allow at least half an hour to warm up your horse. This gets the stiffness out of its joints and helps it move easily.

2 The show
This is your chance to let the judge see how well-schooled and obedient your horse is. Try to be calm and confident.

STRIPPING OFF

If the judge wants to see your horse without its saddle, take off the saddle, saddle pad, and martingale (if it wears one). Wait for an assistant to join you in the ring with a body brush and a stable rubber. Brush out the saddle mark. The judge will want to see your horse led away from and toward him or her. Make sure you take the reins over your horse's head to do this. You must also hold your horse steady while the judge examines it.

THE JUDGE

Your attitude toward the judge is something you develop in your first few shows. It's best not to argue with the judge's decision. All show judging is different and a lot depends on whether the judge likes your sort of horse. Always smile and thank the judge before you leave the ring.

Show jumping

This is the most popular form of competitive riding. It is available at many different levels and can be held inside or outside. It is enjoyed equally by novice and experienced riders. Most ponies and horses seem to enjoy it as much as their owners.

THE COURSE

Indoor show jumping usually has tricky, twisty courses in a small arena. Outdoor arenas usually have a free-flowing course with fewer sharp turns. All course designers try to build a course that will produce perhaps ten clear-rounds, a jump-off against the clock, and corners that can be cut.

finish

start

first-round route

jump-off route

Monday
I didn't really understand what unrated jumping was. Then my instructor, Gerry, explained that it was for people like us whose ponies are not registered jumping ponies. In rated jumping, the rules are really strict. I think Oscar and I will stick to unrated.

WALK THE COURSE

Never be tempted to skip this preparation for show jumping. Once you're in the ring, it's easy to lose your way. Walking the course helps you remember where all the jumps are. It also

gives you an idea of any problems you might come across, so that you can decide how to tackle them. In combinations (two jumps placed close together), pace out the distance between the two jumps. Then ask an experienced person to help you work out whether you should kick your horse on at one point, or let it take an extra stride between the two jumps.

Q How should I warm up for show jumping?

A As you get to know your horse, you will find out how much warmup it requires. If there is plenty of room at the show, it might be best to take your horse away from the other horses. Do some quiet flatwork, such as walking, trotting, and a few circles in both directions. Usually one or two practice jumps are set up in the warmup ring (the ring outside the jumping ring). Just before your round, it is worth popping your horse over these once or twice. Never spend too much time on practice jumps and don't make them too high.

seat

cantle

knee roll

THE JUMP SADDLE

If you do a lot of show jumping, it might be worth buying a special jumping saddle. It is designed to be used with shorter stirrup leathers and has a forward-cut saddle flap. This often has extra padding, called a knee roll. The seat tends to be shallower and the cantle lower than on a general-purpose saddle. You will still need a general-purpose saddle for hacking and other riding.

Always Remember:

Pack your studs. You may need them to give your horse extra grip if the competition is in an outside arena. Pointed studs are used on hard ground. Square, chunky studs are used when it's muddy. As well as studs, you need a T-tap for cleaning the stud-hole in the shoe. You'll also need a wrench for tightening the stud, and petroleum jelly to lubricate the stud-hole before you put in the stud.

Don't forget to take out the studs as soon as the competition is over.

Petroleum jelly

Studs   T-tap

Evening
In a competition yesterday there was a jump with trays of water under the poles. There were yellow plastic ducks floating in them! Oscar stood and stared at them for ages— we ended up being eliminated.

17

Sunday
Gerry gave us copies of a dressage test and told us to learn it. So Annabel and I marked out a dressage arena in the field and practiced on foot until we really knew the test. Now let's see how Oscar manages!

Dressage

There is nothing mystical about dressage. It is just a way of training your horse or pony to carry out basic movements fluently, calmly, and obediently. Any type of horse will improve with schooling, and a well-schooled horse is a pleasure to ride.

K   E   H

The dressage arena
A standard arena is 131 by 66 ft (40 by 20 m) and you can mark it out on any flat ground. You can paint the letters on cones or old paint cans. Place them as shown here. The letters K, H, M, and F should be 20 ft (6 m) from the corners on the long sides. In a dressage test, the rider always enters at A. The center of the arena is known as X.

A   C

F   B   M

DRESSAGE SADDLE

This saddle isn't very comfortable for everyday riding, but it does get you into the correct position for dressage. It has a very deep seat and a straight-cut flap. The girth straps hanging below the panel show that it is meant to be used with a short girth. This stops the girth buckle from lying under your thigh.

CLOTHING FOR DRESSAGE

For dressage you should be clean and tidy, just as you are for showing. You should also wear gloves. Spurs and a whip are allowed. Your horse should also be well-groomed with its mane braided. Make sure your horse isn't wearing any boots,

bandages, a saddle cloth, a colored browband, or anything else fancy. Don't be afraid to ask the organizer of a dressage competition if you are unsure of the dress rules.

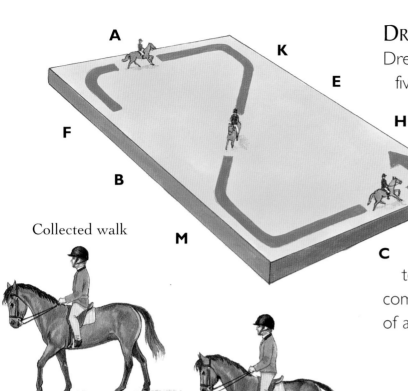

DRESSAGE TESTS

Dressage tests usually last about five minutes. They include different movements and paces for you and your horse to perform in a particular order. You have to do several changes of pace and direction. You can get a copy of the test from the event organizer. Dressage tests are specially written for dressage competitions and for the dressage section of a one-day event.

Collected walk

Working trot

I got my first dressage score sheet back. It wasn't great, but the comments were very helpful. I'll do better next time.

Q How is dressage scored?

A All dressage tests are divided into sections. Each section contains one or more movements, such as a change of rein. You are given marks out of ten for each section. A score of five or more is a passing grade. These marks are recorded on your score sheet, along with any comments the judge makes. Marks are also given for the overall performance of both you and your horse. In a dressage competition, the competitor with the highest mark is the winner. In combined training (dressage and show jumping) and one-day events, the final mark is the number of penalties given. Penalties are given for any mistakes you make. So in these cases, the lower the score the better.

Extended trot

Medium canter

DRESSAGE PACES

All of the movements that you do at junior level dressage are relatively easy for the average horse or pony. The paces are simply what you would normally do in basic schooling. When riding your test, try to concentrate on accuracy, smooth transitions from one gait to another, and getting your horse to bend when turning a circle. In many competitions you will be expected to perform the test from memory.

One-day event

This is a very popular event and is a true test of your horse's all-around ability. It combines the discipline of dressage, the stamina of cross-country jumping, and the accuracy and timing of the show-jumping ring. It is organized at all levels, from novice to experienced.

My first one-day event was a DISASTER. I fell off on the cross-country course and then went on the wrong side of a flag!

DRESSAGE

This is always the first of the three parts of a one-day event. The score that you get is the dressage penalty score. So you want it to be as low as possible.

Stream

Tires

SHOW JUMPING

This usually takes place after the cross-country. It is an ordinary show-jumping course. Any penalties that you get are added to the dressage score.

Finish

Tiger trap

Start

CHECKING THE COURSE

A map of the cross-country course is always displayed. Study it carefully before your turn. The time allowed to complete the course is also given, and you will get time penalties if you exceed it.

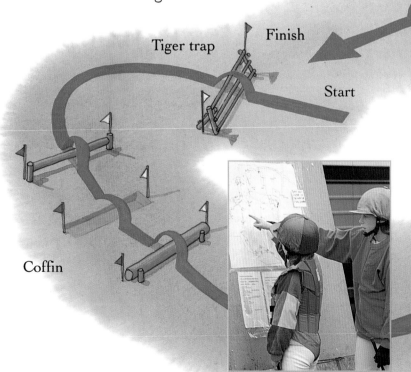

Coffin

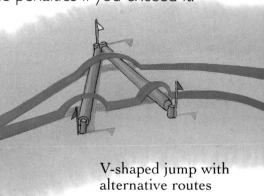

V-shaped jump with alternative routes

WATER JUMPS

Only experienced riders have to jump into or out of water, but you might be asked to splash through water and perhaps to jump a fence at the other side. If your horse hates water, some courses provide a learner fence to jump instead of going through the water.

BODY PROTECTORS

All cross-country riders should wear body protectors. These are specially designed, padded tabards that absorb shock and protect your spine, ribs, and shoulders. You should have your body protector properly fitted by a trained supplier.

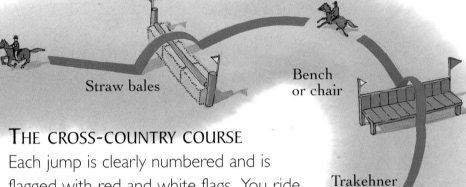

Straw bales

Bench or chair

Trakehner

THE CROSS-COUNTRY COURSE

Each jump is clearly numbered and is flagged with red and white flags. You ride between the flags. The red flag must be on your right and the white one on your left. Some jumps have more than one route. The shorter, direct route is often much more difficult.

Puzzle with alternative routes

Always Remember:

Plan the timing of your cross-country ride carefully. As you walk the course, note the places where you have to go slowly because of difficult ground. Just as importantly, note the places where you are able to speed up. This will help you to know where to make up some time if you feel that you are falling behind. Look carefully at each jump. In particular, decide which route you are going to take on those jumps that have more than one route. Does your horse like water? If not, then look to see whether or not there is a learner fence you can jump instead.

Transportation

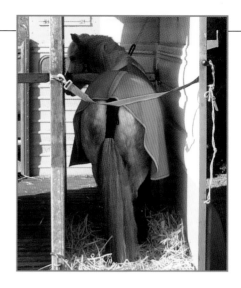

Not many riders hack to shows because of the amount of traffic on the roads. Once you start competing regularly you will need to use a horse trailer. This gives you the chance to take part in different events over interesting and varied courses.

TRAVEL PROTECTION

Travel clothing guards against knocks and keeps your horse clean for the show. Horses usually wear traveling boots. These go from above the knee to just above the hoof. Your horse should also wear a lightweight rug, a tail bandage, and a tail guard. If your horse throws its head up a lot, it is a good idea for it to wear a poll guard on top of its head to prevent injury.

tail bandage

rug

traveling boots

4 pm—I think Oscar must have been fed in a trailer when he was young, because I never have any problem loading him. In fact, twice he has walked into the trailer on his own while I was talking to Annabel!

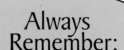

Always Remember:

Clean the trailer after you have used it. If the floor is wet, remove any straw and leave the ramps down so that air can circulate and allow the floor to dry. It is most important for your horse's safety that the floor should not rot. Cleaning and drying it should prevent this. Don't clean out your trailer while you are still at the show —it is very annoying for the owner of the field.

THE TRAILER

A two-horse trailer is the most popular kind of trailer as it lets your horse travel with a companion. Trailers with a front and a rear ramp are good, as your horse doesn't have to be backed out. This can make it less frightening for a nervous horse. Always load your horse by calmly walking in a straight line up the ramp. Tie up your horse with quite a short length of rope.

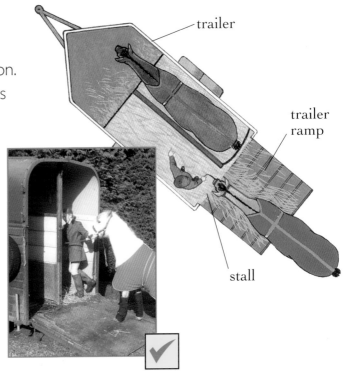

trailer

trailer ramp

stall

partition

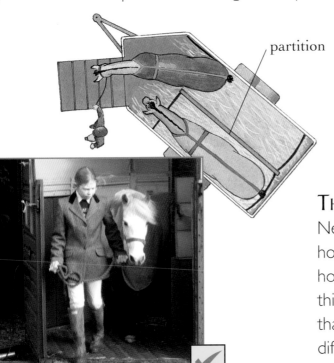

THE WRONG WAY

Never try to load your horse as shown here. Your horse will win a battle like this because it is stronger than you. If your horse is difficult to load, ask an experienced person for help.

Q What do I need to know about hacking to a show?

A If the route is a safe one and you do not have big roads to cross or to ride along, hacking can be fun. Plan your route beforehand so that you know exactly which way to go. Take a head-collar with you, either on your horse or buckled around your waist. Allow plenty of time and enjoy the trip. It is best to travel with friends. At the showground, find a shady spot where you can tie up your horse. It helps if someone else can bring things like your grooming kit in the car.

Extra schooling

There is nothing like a competition for showing up basic problems, either yours or your horse's. Either way, there is only one solution—you both have to go back to school. If possible, get a good instructor to help you smooth out the rough patches.

Losing

Losing is hard to take. The most important thing to do is to accept defeat gracefully. Go away, do some schooling, and come back to do your best at the next show. Remember that entering competitions is all about enjoying yourself. It isn't just the winning that is important.

Grid work

Getting back to basics is a good way to improve your chances at the next show. If your horse is rushing its jumps and not following your commands, however hard you try, you need to go back to the very beginning. Walk your horse calmly over poles on the ground. Then progress slowly to a grid of small jumps.

Make a video
One of the most helpful ways of improving your riding is to get a friend to videotape you during a schooling session. Until you see yourself riding, it can be difficult to tell just what you are doing wrong.

Don't try to advance too quickly, or all the old problems will come back. It is important to get your horse going steadily for you, answering to your legs and voice. Soon you will be able to complete a course of jumps without any problems.

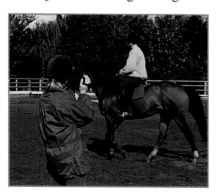

BAD POSITION

It is important to keep a contact with your horse's mouth through the reins. This rider (near right) has reins that are too long. He has little control of his horse. The other rider (far right) is being left behind as the horse goes over the jump. Help your horse by sitting in the correct position and giving clear instructions.

Jumping too early

Oscar is turning into a really good jumper. I think he is enjoying it, because his ears always prick up when we enter the ring.

JUMPING PROBLEMS

Both the problems illustrated here show that you need to help your horse know when to take off. In the first, the horse has taken off too soon and will need to stretch out too far to clear the jump. In the second, a late takeoff means the horse knocks the jump down. With practice you can learn to recognize your horse's stride and when it should take off.

Jumping too late

FLATWORK

Flatwork is the most important part of training. By doing flatwork you will be able to do more exciting activities, like jumping, more efficiently, safely, and successfully. Try to spend a short time each day on schooling on the flat until your horse is moving out confidently. As you improve, gradually introduce more advanced movements. Make sure you keep having lessons with an experienced instructor.

Unusual activities

There are many different types of competition to enter and lots of ways to enjoy your horse. Here are some of the fun things that you can take part in. If you ask around, you may be able to join a group or club in your area.

Cross-country riding

TETRATHLON

This is a four-part event organized by the Pony Club. The competition usually takes place over two days. It creates a great feeling of team spirit and you are likely to make many friends. The four parts include riding over a cross-country course, shooting with a .177 air pistol, cross-country running over a certain distance, and swimming as far as you can in a certain number of minutes. The older you are, the further or longer the races will be. Usually, the shooting and swimming take place on the first day and riding and running are held on the second. The points you get for each event are added together to determine the winner.

Tuesday
Annabel and I had an invitation to learn all about tetrathlon. We were given a chance to shoot and shown exactly how to stand and hold the pistol. I completely missed the target with my first shot, but I soon learned not to wait too long before lining up and firing. I think it's another thing that you just get better and better at with practice!

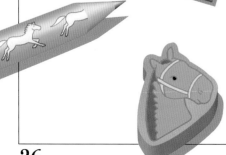

Race information

- Riding — 1-1½ mi (1,600-2,500 m) cross-country
- Running — 1,100-3,300 yards (1,000-3,000 m)
- Swimming — points are scored for every length you swim for 2-3 minutes
- Shooting — 10 shots at two targets from 23-33 ft (7-10 m)

roping horn

Western bridle

long leather stirrups

WESTERN RIDING

Western riders use a specially designed saddle and bridle. A Western saddle has a roping horn, a high cantle, and long leather stirrups. It is heavier than an ordinary saddle and the horse is gradually introduced to it. You sit deep in the saddle and ride with long stirrup leathers. This allows you to sit in the saddle for a long time without getting too tired. This is useful for cowboys who spend many hours in the saddle. You hold the reins with one hand and use neck-reining to steer the horse.

Lunchtime I thought I might take up endurance riding and went for a really long three-hour ride. Oscar was fine when we got back, but I was so exhausted I could hardly stand. Perhaps endurance riding can wait!

ENDURANCE RIDING

Endurance riding is competing over long distances to be completed as efficiently as possible without distress to your horse. At various points along the route, your horse is examined by a veterinarian before you're allowed to continue. You are also met by an assistant who gives you and your horse whatever help or refreshment you need.

Q What is the difference between the tetrathlon and the modern pentathlon?

A The modern pentathlon consists of riding, shooting, running, swimming, and fencing. Tetrathlon doesn't include fencing. Most pentathletes start their career in the Pony Club and then take up fencing as they get older. Riding in modern pentathlon is different from tetrathlon because the competitors ride horses that they have never seen before. The riding is usually over a show-jumping course. In tetrathlon, you ride your own horse and you don't do any show jumping. In ordinary athletics, the pentathlon comprises various field and track events and dates back to as long ago as 708 B.C.

Polo

Some horse activities, like polo, go back several centuries or even longer. Others have only been around for a few years. If you ask around, you will find out about many new, exciting things to try, some more difficult than others.

Saturday
Someone asked me if I'd like to join the polo squad, so I went to watch a practice. It looked like fun. The problem is, if I played polo, I wouldn't have time to do much else. Also, you usually have to travel a long way to play in a polo tournament. I'd definitely like to give it a try one day though.

ORIGINS OF POLO
Polo was played as long ago as 500 B.C. It began in Central Asia and had become popular in China by the 700s A.D. The British discovered polo in India around 1850, and it later crossed the Atlantic to America.

goal line

side line

goal posts

40-yard mark

safety zone

starting point

THE GAME
The aim is to hit the ball through your opponents' goal. There are two teams, each with four members. At junior level, games consist of one or two six-minute periods, known as chukkers.

POLOCROSSE

This is a mixture of polo and lacrosse. It's played with special sticks that can scoop up the foam rubber ball. There are six players to a team, but only three are on the field at any one time. Each half of the team plays alternate chukkers. There are between two and eight chukkers in a match. A player is only allowed to ride one horse in a match.

HORSEBALL

In horseball, a goal is scored when the ball is thrown through a net similar to one used in basketball. The ball is about the size of a soccer ball and has leather hand grips on it to make it easier to hold. A goal cannot be scored until all four members of the team have held the ball.

VAULTING

This is a form of gymnastics on horseback. The best type of horse has a broad back and smooth paces. Usually, the horse wears a saddle pad fitted with a roller bar, instead of a saddle. The rider performs various acrobatics while the horse canters around the arena. In some displays, more than one athlete will take part in exercises on one horse. Apart from having a well-trained horse, the rider needs to be very fit and athletic.

2 pm—I think I could get quite interested in polocrosse. There is a group near my house that plays polocrosse, so I could try it. Oh dear! There are so many things Oscar and I could do, but there just aren't enough hours in the day.

Quiz Time

Can you remember what you have learned in this book? Test yourself and your friends by trying this quiz.

1 What is useful for making your horse's white socks look whiter?

2 What does a warmup ring steward do in a jumping competition?

3 Why is neck-reining useful in gymkhana games?

4 How much room should you leave between you and the horse in front when riding around a show ring?

5 How big is a standard dressage arena?

6 Starting with A and moving clockwise around the dressage arena, write down the letters in their correct order.

7 In a cross-country competition, which colored flag should be on your right?

8 Which events make up the tetrathlon?

9 What is the term given to the period of play in polo?

Useful addresses

U.S.A. Pony Clubs
4041 Iron Works
    Parkway
Lexington KY 40511-8462
www.ponyclub.org
Tel: (859) 254-7669

U.S.A. Equestrian, Inc.
4047 Iron Works
    Parkway
Lexington KY 40511-8463
www.equestrian.org
Tel: (859) 254-2476

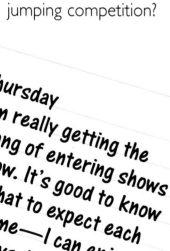

Thursday
I'm really getting the hang of entering shows now. It's good to know what to expect each time—I can enjoy myself even more!

Answers

1 Chalk 2 He or she takes the competitor's number, marks the order of jumping, and makes sure the riders are ready for their turn. 3 It leaves you one hand free for holding equipment. 4 At least one horse's length 5 131 ft by 66 ft (40 m by 20 m) 6 A, K, E, H, C, M, B, F 7 The red flag 8 Shooting, swimming, running, and riding 9 Chukker.

Glossary

bending race
Gymkhana game in which competitors weave through a row of poles.

body protector
Specially padded garment worn to protect a rider in a fall.

chukker
Period of play in polo and polocrosse.

class
Each show is split into classes. You choose which classes to enter. Different classes are designed for different abilities and age groups.

dressage test
Set of movements to be performed by each rider in a dressage competition.

figure-eight
Movement performed in shape of an eight to demonstrate a horse's agility.

hunter trials
Cross-country competition.

knee roll
Padded area at the front of the saddle flap on a jumping saddle.

neat's-foot oil
Substance that can be painted onto leather to keep it supple.

neck-reining
Guiding the horse with only one hand on the reins.

pentathlon
Five-part competition including shooting, swimming, running, riding, and fencing.

poll guard
A covering that protects the part of a horse's head between its ears.

polo
Game played on horseback with mallet-shaped sticks.

salute
Gesture made by a rider to tell the judge that they have finished their display.

schedule
List of classes in a show or cross-country event.

stripping off
Taking off your horse's saddle so that the show judge can see the shape of your horse.

tetrathlon
Four-part competition consisting of shooting, swimming, running, and riding.

traveling boots
Padded leggings that stretch from above the knee to the hoof, used when traveling.

T-tap
Wrench used for cleaning stud holes and tightening studs.

vaulting
1) Gymnastics on horseback
2) Leaping onto a horse, particularly in mounted games.

walking the course
Going on foot around a show-jumping or a cross-country course.

warmup ring
Area at the entrance to a showing or jumping ring where competitors gather.

Index

Photo credits

Abbreviations: l-left, r-right, b-bottom, t-top, c-center, m-middle

Front and back cover, 1, 4tr, 5bl, 5br, 6mr all, 7ml, 7br, 8c, 9bm, 10br, 11c, 14tr both, 16mr, 18bm, 21tl, 21tr, 22 both, 23 all, 24c, 25bl, 26tr, 30tl, 31ml, 32bl—Select Pictures. 3b, 9br, 16ml, 20ml, 20c, 27tl, 27bm, 28br, 29bm, 32tr—Corel. 4c, 5c, 8t, 12c, 13tl, 13c, 15br, 24bl, 27ml, 29mr—Horsepix. 4br, 7tr all, 8mr, 9tl, 9bl, 10c, 10bm, 10bl, 11t, 12br, 15ml, 15c, 16ml, 20b, 29ml—Kit Houghton Photography. 6ml, 14br, 24br—Aubrey Wade.